Contents

	About The Author	iii
	How To Use 'The Handbook To Affiliate Marketing'	vi
1.	What is Affiliate Marketing	1
2.	A Glossary Of Affiliate Marketing Terms	9
3.	What You Need To Get Started With Affiliate Marketing	14
4.	Features To Look For In An Affiliate Program	19
5.	How To Select The Best Affiliate Product For Your Blog	25
6.	Top Affiliate Networks/Marketplaces	35
7.	The Art Of Promoting An Affiliate Product On Your Blog	38
8.	How Google Treats Affiliate Links For Search Engine Ranking	46
9.	How You Can Effectively Increase Affiliate Sales	49

10.	How To Start Using ShareASale Affiliate Marketplace & Make Money	53
11.	How To Using The Amazon Affiliate Program & Start Making Money	59
12.	Other Affiliate Marketplaces	76
13.	Affiliate or AdSense: Which is Better?	78
14.	CPA vs. Affiliate Marketing: A Beginner's Guide To CPA Marketing	85
15.	Best Recurring Affiliate Programs	90
16.	FAQs About Affiliate Marketing	99

About The Author

Harsh Agrawal for The Week Magazine Photo Shoot.

Howdy mate,

I'm Harsh Agrawal, and you will be spending the next few

hours with me reading one of my finest works. I will be passing on as much knowledge to you as possible about affiliate marketing. You can think of me as a coach or a friend or just someone with nearly a decade of experience in the field.

But before we do that, let me quickly give you my background and then we can start learning **everything** you need to know about starting a career in affiliate marketing.

Don't mistake the word 'career' here for a 9 to 5 job. It implies becoming your own boss and earning more than what you would make in a corporate job.

I'm someone who does just a few things, but I put my heart and soul into them. I love blogging and have always had a passion for making this world a better place. I would never have imagined in my wildest dreams that I would become a professional blogger and live a dream life (more on it later). To be honest, until 2008, I didn't think it was *even possible* to earn money online.

I was awestruck when someone sent me **$10 via PayPal** for a task I performed online. That changed everything. My take on earning money online had changed.

My online career started in 2006 with a popular Orkut community and in 2008 I started ShoutMeLoud.com **(SML) that become my first domain name**. In the last 10 years, it has grown to become the *world's community & learning source for existing & aspiring bloggers.*

At ShoutMeLoud, one can learn **everything** there is to know about how to earn passive income online and even how to live a boss-free life.

A great part of this book is inspired by earlier work on SML.

Some of the popular topics covered on SML are:

- How to launch your own blog and make money from it
- Learn SEO
- Learn Digital marketing
- Complete WordPress training (Basic & Advanced)
- How to become a better human being

The last topic is a little offbeat but the fact is you can't be successful without being a good person. We all are born with our positives and negatives. Acquiring skills to be a happy person, or a good conversation starter, or a leader, fighting our negatives etc. are just one of many aspects of becoming a better person.

I decided to add this offbeat topic to ShoutMeLoud (SML) because it is essential for you and me to develop into a better human being and enjoy what life has to offer us. We will talk more about the ideology of ShoutMeLoud but for now, let me finish my introduction so that we can start talking about the skills that have the power to transform your life.

I'm just an ordinary guy who lives life to the fullest. I love traveling. You can describe me as a "happy-go-lucky" character. I like to talk about things related to marketing, entrepreneurship, and the art of living. I'm not a very serious person but I love to talk about big ideas.

If you share similar qualities, feel free to join me on Facebook.

In *"The Handbook to Affiliate Marketing "*, I have shared and compiled everything I have learned about affiliate marketing thus far. This book is *often updated* with new information and you are **entitled to free updates** for all upcoming versions for the next one year.

How To Use 'The Handbook To Affiliate Marketing'

This book is for a wide range of audience. It is as much for a beginner as it is for someone highly skilled at affiliate marketing.

If you have never taken a dip in the world of affiliate marketing, you will learn *everything you need* to help you get started.

If you have made a few affiliate sales in the past, you should be able to increase your sales **substantially** if you pay close attention to the details I have shared in this book.

I will help you understand everything there is to know about affiliate marketing, along with essential tips, tricks, and trade secrets.

You can read about these techniques, **but the most important thing is**:

- You *need* to start *practicing* these techniques *every day*.

First tip:

If you learn how to get more sales, you can *copy the same formula* for any product in any niche.

Cool, right?

Well, then you're ready to get started and jump into the sea of affiliate marketing.

The big question:

CAN THIS BOOK REALLY HELP YOU MAKE MONEY?

Yes, it can!

But that can only happen if you are willing to dedicate the next few days to test it out thoroughly. All I ask from you is to have **determination and patience** when implementing the strategies listed in this book.

Instead of comparing your work with others, you need to focus on yourself! You will also be honing many of your skills in the coming days that will *help you enjoy* everything that this book has to offer.

I have gotten a lot of feedback on this book, and many readers have indeed confirmed that this book has helped them make money.

However, some readers also *failed* to make money. The percentage of such users is meager, but there have been cases where people have been unable to make the most of this book.

And that, my friends, is because people think of affiliate marketing as a *'get rich quick' scheme.*

It is not.

Affiliate marketing is *undoubtedly the right way* to earn *huge* amounts of income online, but it takes **time**, **dedication**, **consistency**, and **undivided attention**.

As a beginner, *an hour a day* is good enough to get rolling. However, whatever little time you invest should be productive. Only then will you learn more with time. Consistency is the key.

The more time you spend learning about affiliate marketing

and its complementary skills (*like managing a virtual team*), the more it is **guaranteed** to be fruitful for you.

But you will also find that learning all of this is fun!

There's no need for head scratching because I will help you out with **detailed blueprints and guides** that will assist you in your learning. *I will also send you emails for further understanding in the coming days.*

Before we start, to clear up the doubt, check out what previous readers have said after applying the techniques mentioned in this book:

Always remember: If one person can do it, you can do it too

What is Affiliate Marketing

Affiliate marketing is one of the coolest ways to earn money from blogging or online marketing. Once you have done the hard work, you can make money even when you are **sleeping** (or scuba diving).

Me in Bali: 2016

Affiliate marketing is one of the oldest forms of marketing. In technical terms, here is the definition:

> *– Affiliates recommend products, and when someone purchases those products, affiliates earn a portion of the sale.*

You have probably seen this business model in the real-estate business. In today's times where almost everything is digital, the same form of business conducted online is called "affiliate marketing".

You can earn anywhere from $1 to $5000 a day depending on what products you promote and recommend. What makes affiliate marketing so lucrative is the fact that once you have covered the **basics**, i.e., putting your content online, creating a system, and driving traffic, the money keeps flowing in.

I will discuss more on this later but for now, review this image to understand the basic model of affiliate marketing:

online shopper

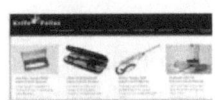
affiliate site

merchant site

Explanation

01 Online shopper decides to buy an item

02 He lands on an affiliate site

03 He is now redirected to the merchants site

04 The shopper finally makes the purchase and the merchant rewards the affiliate for his effort

ShoutMeLoud.com

From the image:

1. A shopper/reader clicks on a product link on **your website**.
2. Shopper lands on the **merchant's website.**
3. The shopper purchases the product.
4. You earn a portion of that sale.

You must be thinking as to how companies know if the sale is coming from your link and not from someone else's.

The answer:

- **A tracking link** (a.k.a *affiliate link*)

Don't get confused with the jargon just yet. "Tracking Link" is pretty simple.

It is a **unique link** given *only to you* by the affiliate/product company. **This unique tracking link** is used to keep track of all the traffic you send (and sales you make) via your website or other promotion channels.

A tracking link is like any other URL, but contains a *unique* string/parameter for your profile. When you join an affiliate program, you get your tracking link from the affiliate dashboard.

Here are two examples of such tracking links:

- https://www.tubebuddy.com/Shout
- **http://click.tunnelbear.com/aff_c?offer_id=2&aff_id=1314**

I know the second tracking link in the above example *looks visually horrible*.

Don't worry. You will **soon** learn how to make your *ugly links look pretty*.

These two links are *my affiliate links* for two different affiliate programs.

When you join an affiliate program, you get *your affiliate link*. All you need to do is promote those links using legitimate methods, and when someone purchases the product, you earn a commission!

Each link is personalized to enable the company to track your referrals.

For example:

Tubebuddy.com/Shout (*my unique affiliate link*)

Tubebuddy.com/somekeyword (*your unique link*)

TubeBuddy (A tool for YouTube) has an affiliate program where they pay 30% of commission per sale. You can create a free account by going to www.tubebuddy.com .

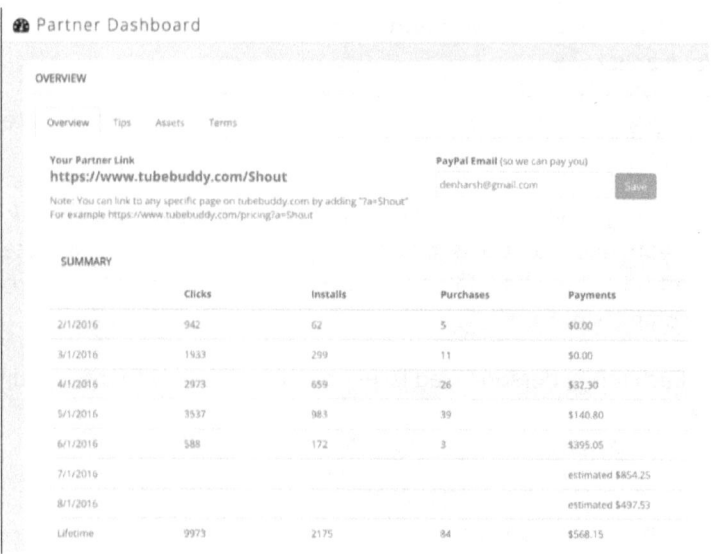

Here's another question: *"What if companies don't pay or don't show a real sale as a sale?"*

Answer:

- Well, unfortunately, that does happen **a lot of time** and that is where this guide will help you learn how to avoid such situations and scam affiliate companies.

In an upcoming chapter, I will tell you about affiliate marketplaces where you can find **reliable companies** and form an authentic affiliate partnership.

(Note: Many old-fashioned affiliate programs, instead of using affiliate URLs, let a buyer add the email ID of referrals (i.e., you). That too is accounted for in an affiliate sale. However, this is not the best way to track progress. More on that later.)

Alright, things get interesting from here:

There are **many ways** for you to join an affiliate program. In this book, I will discuss the *two most popular* and effective ways to join affiliate programs.

1. Joining an **affiliate marketplace**
2. Joining a **direct affiliate program** (Tricks on finding such programs in a later chapter)

Websites that sell products online such as Amazon, Shopify, GoPro etc, *usually* offer an affiliate program. When you sign up for their affiliate program (*free*), you gain access to their affiliate dashboard where you can find *your unique tracking link*.

In a later section of this book, I will share tricks to discover affiliate programs in **every niche**.

Here are some of the widely used promotion methods by affiliate marketers:

- Blogging or Content Marketing
- YouTube videos
- Instagram, Facebook, Twitter
- PPC Marketing (Facebook ads, AdWords ads)
- Buying paid traffic
- Email Marketing
- Creating a 'coupon & deals' website
- Creating cashback website

Note: *I have shared tricks to find more of these affiliate programs later in this book. Stay glued!*

Every affiliate program has their specific Terms of Standards (TOS).

For example, many of them offer a **60-day cookie period**. It means that the company will pay you commission even if a visitor, who used your affiliate link to land on a company's page, purchases a product or service within **60 days** (on the same device) and not immediately.

Another interesting thing to know:

- You will get paid for *other product purchases as well*.

For example, if your reader goes to Amazon.com using your affiliate link and purchases **another product which you haven't recommended**, you will still get the *same commission out of that sale*.

Pro Tip: Most companies *require* you to have a blog or a website for becoming their affiliate partner. It helps them get serious people and helps you too because having your blog/website is **one of the best ways** to make an affiliate sale.

You can follow this tutorial (https://www.shoutmeloud.com/how-to-install-wordpress-and-steps-after-installing-wordpress.html) *to launch your blog.*

A Glossary Of Affiliate Marketing Terms

Now, let's understand some of the common terminologies in the affiliate marketing industry. You will come across these words **every time** you learn something about "Affiliate Marketing" or "Digital Marketing".

- **Affiliates:** Publishers (like you and me) who join an affiliate program.

- **Affiliate Marketplace:** This is a marketplace where you can find numerous companies offering affiliate programs for their product(s). There are many marketplaces (like ShareASale, Commission Junction, JvZoo, ClickBank, etc.) which work as a central database for affiliate programs in different niches. **This one is important**, as using the above sites will help you find affiliate programs for your niche. I have written more about the marketplaces mentioned above in a further section of this Affiliate Marketing Handbook.

- **Affiliate Software:** Softwares used by companies to create an in-house affiliate program for their product (this may not be as important at this stage, but it's always good to be knowledgeable). Example: iDevaffiliate, HasOffers.

• **Affiliate Link:** Unique tracking link offered by your affiliate program to track the progress of your affiliate promotion. (We have already discussed this earlier.)

• **Affiliate ID:** This is similar to an affiliate link. In some cases, many affiliate programs offer a "unique ID" which you can later **add to any page of the product site** (example: productpage.com/AffiliateID).

•**Payment Mode/Method:** Different affiliate programs offer different methods of payment. Common payment modes include a check, wire transfer, PayPal, Payoneer, and others.

◦ **PayPal:** This is the *most common* payment method to receiving affiliate earnings. You need to create a PayPal account if you don't already have one. You can follow this guide (https://www.shoutmeloud.com/indian-paypal-verification.html) to create your account. Companies will send your payment through PayPal from where it is transferable to your bank account.

◦ **Payoneer:** This is another payment program that you may use to receive affiliate commissions. Payoneer offers a Master Card, and you can use it as a *debit card*. You can also transfer money from Payoneer to your bank account. You can join Payoneer at www.payoneer.com/in/.

◦ **Wire transfer:** Many companies offer direct deposit, and whenever possible, you should prefer this method as this will *save you a lot of money*. When you use PayPal or Payoneer, you will be paying a small amount as service charge. With wire transfer (ACH), you will *not be liable to pay any service fee*.

  ◦ **Check:** I know it's funny to hear that some companies do not offer digital payments. One such company, Aweber (popular email-marketing system), offers affiliate payments via paper check only. I find this outrageous, but at times, we can't do much but follow the company's guidelines to get paid.

  ◦ **Bitcoins:** Starting 2018, a lot of companies have started offering payments in Bitcoins. There are only a handful of such companies but you should be ready to receive payments in Bitcoins. You can head to Coinsutra.com to learn more about Bitcoins and other stuff related to cryptocurrencies.

• **Affiliate Manager:** When you join an affiliate program (directly or using a marketplace), there is always an affiliate manager associated. Affiliate managers are *central to many things. You should always build a good relationship with your affiliate managers*. They will help you get increased commissions and also give you a heads-up about new offers.

• **Commission Percentage/Amount:** The amount or percentage of commission you will get for every sale via your affiliate link. Many companies offer a fixed percentage of the sale amount (for example 30%) while others provide fixed rates per sale (say $25).

• **Two-Tier Affiliate Marketing:** This is an excellent way of making money from an affiliate program. In this, you *recommend others* to join a particular affiliate program and earn a *commission when your sub-affiliates generate sales*. This is like MLM (multi-level marketing) but in a **legitimate way**. This is also popularly known as *Sub-Affiliate Commissions*.

• **Landing Page:** A unique product sales/demo page which is used to increase sales. The purpose of the landing page is to direct *traffic to take a desired action*. It could be as simple as *subscribing to your email newsletter* or *buying a product*. You can learn more when I finish my next book on *Email Marketing*, but for now you need to know that *landing pages are very useful*. You can use software like LeadPages to create a professional landing page.

• **Custom/Special Affiliate Offer:** Many companies usually have special offers for their affiliate partners who give them good sales numbers. These affiliates are called *"Super Affiliates"*. You should focus on being one of them.

• **Link Cloaking:** Most affiliate tracking links are ugly. Link cloaking allows you to turn ugly looking links into easily readable and attractive links. I have shared the *complete tutorial* on link cloaking in a later part of this Book.

• **Custom Coupons:** Many programs let affiliates create custom coupons, which is *also used to track sales*. Also, custom discount coupons help you *increase* affiliate sales. If you are one that generates impressive sales figures for any particular merchant, you can always ask the affiliate managers to provide you with an *exclusive coupon code* which also helps in the *branding* of your service/blog/website.

ADVERTISING/AFFILIATE MARKETING TERMS:

In the below section you will learn some *more terms* which are related to advertising within the affiliate industry.

Understanding these terms will help you to pick the **right affiliate offers** from various networks.

- **EPC (earning per click):** This is calculated by taking the amount of clicks divided by the commission earned.

- **CPC (cost per click):** The *actual price* you pay per click. This is a common term when running PPC campaigns using AdWords or Facebook advertising.

- **CR (conversion rate):** Conversions divided by clicks. This gives you an idea of how your ad campaigns are performing.

Note: An online company gets benefit from an affiliate program, as this is one of the best ways to get free promotion and save on advertising.

It also benefits the affiliate.

Whenever you see coupons or discounted products offered via links, most of the time, these links are affiliate links. When you make a purchase, webmasters make money.

It's a win-win-win scenario!

Don't be shy to use other's affiliate links, as they have worked hard to educate you on something. By using their affiliate link, **you are rewarding them**. You will understand this better once you start working on content generation & educating your audience.

What You Need To Get Started With Affiliate Marketing

I will now share with you all the essential topics to become a **master at affiliate marketing.** But first, let's take some *baby steps* which will help you to get the basics right.

One can begin affiliate marketing using any form of digital marketing.

Examples of affiliate websites:

- A blog which educates readers
- Coupon-based site
- Product comparison site
- Niche Amazon site (designed specifically for Amazon affiliate earnings)

Other techniques:

- PPC marketing (via Facebook ads or Google AdWords)
- Email marketing
    - typically used with blogging or PPC but can be done separately

Note: These are some popular methods used by affiliate marketers. Remember, it is not limited to just what is listed above. Once you master this course, you can discover your medium for affiliate marketing.

I prefer educating users and recommending products **that I use** or have used in the past. Once you learn the in's & out's of affiliate marketing, you can use any of the ways mentioned above (or many other ways) to start making money.

Typically, **I suggest blogging** because you will not only be making money, you will also be *making a name for yourself*. That's more of my personal choice, but whatever method you use is ultimately a decision you should be happy with.

Tips for non-writers:

If you are not into content writing, you should consider using other forms of promotional methods other than blogging.

But if you want to create a blog and don't want to write, a good workaround is **hiring a content writer** from sites like ContentMart, TextBroker or PeoplePerHour.

My only suggestion is **don't promote anything that you would not recommend to your loved ones**. For example a *sketchy poker site or untested health-related products.*

Again, this is a decision you need to make based on your moral conscience.

LINK CLOAKING: YOUR NEW BEST FRIEND

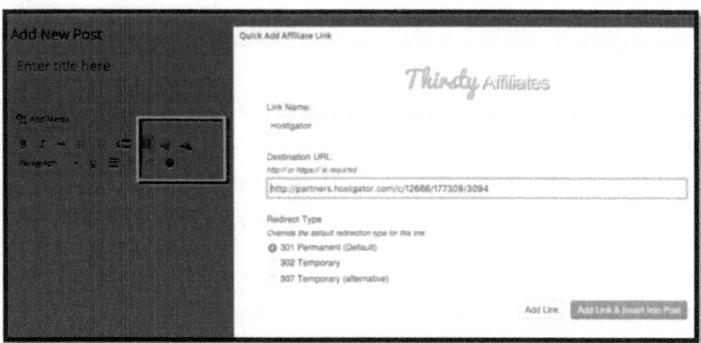

Link cloaking, in simple words, means making long affiliate URLs into shorter and prettier ones. We do this for multiple reasons.

Transforming the ugly looking URLs:

Usually, affiliate links you get from your affiliate programs are not very pleasing to the eye. They are a long strand of numbers, letters, and symbols. Link cloaking turns these long, confusing links into short, crisp, good-looking links.

This technique can also add your brand name into the URL which makes it more trustworthy and brands you as a reputable source.

Here's an example:

Affiliate URL:

http://www.semrush.com/billing/offers/buy/4kprox41?promo=SHOUTMELOUD-R4EQ4OIZ

Affiliate Cloaked URL:

http://affiliatemarketing.buzz/go/SEMRUSH/

Uncloaked link

http://www.amazon.in/gp/product/
B0154LXZVA/ref=br_asw_pdt
-3?pf_rd_m=A1VBAL9TL5
WCBF&pf_rd_s

Cloaked link

ShoutMeLoud.com/go/affiliate

Notice that the second link looks better, more organized, and branded. Instead of just using an affiliate link in its default form, it's better to make it look more professional with cloaking.

Why You Should Always Cloak Your Links?

Search Engine Ranking:

One of the major concerns with affiliate marketers is search engine ranking. Most affiliate marketers miss out on optimizing their blog and fail to ensure that their blog is SEO friendly.

Cloaking your URLs helps optimize your site.

Changing Future URLs:

At times, your product company may change their affiliate

software which requires you to change your affiliate URLs *everywhere*. When you are using a link cloaking solution, you can change *all URLs with a single click*.

- *Pro Tip*: Whenever I add a link to any product which doesn't yet have an affiliate program, I still **cloak the normal URL** so that in the future I can easily update the URL with an affiliate link when it becomes available. *Just using this technique helped me earn thousands of dollars extra/month*.

Affiliate URLs are banned on many sites:

On many popular sites such as Facebook, or even using PPC on Google, affiliate URLs are **banned**. Link cloaking helps you eradicate this issue.

Links to Link Cloaking:

- If you are using the WordPress platform for your blog or website, you can use this popular plugin: ThirstyAffiliate WordPress plugin.
- For any other platform you can use the Geni.us website.

Features To Look For In An Affiliate Program

In the past decade, I have been an affiliate with **over 90 direct affiliate programs**, and each of them is different in their own way.

They all differ in affiliate policies, payouts, commissions, and *their affinity towards affiliates* like you and me.

I'm going to list down some of the features that will make your affiliate journey easier.

If you join a direct affiliate program where any of the features listed below are not available, you can always **ask your affiliate manager** to add them.

Let's start with #1.

Payment Method:

When you are starting out with affiliate marketing, I suggest you ignore all the fancy features *and focus on the payment method*.

This is particularly true in Asian countries, where many users have shown concerns due to the *limited functionalities of popular services like* **PayPal and** **Payoneer.**

Make sure the company offers a payment method that you can use. In certain situations, payments via check is recommended.

Tasks for this section:

1. Create a PayPal account if you don't have one.
2. Create a Payoneer account if you don't have one.
3. Create a bank account in your city which accepts payment in different currencies. Once you have that bank account, you can use Evernote (or any other note taking app) to keep the following information handy:

- Name:
- Account number:
- Bank Name:
- Address:

Update: Most companies including Amazon, CJ.com, ShareASale now offer direct bank deposits.

Single product affiliate link (Deep linking):

Imagine you sign up for an affiliate program with a lot of products and you can't find a *direct affiliate link* to an individual product. This can be very annoying.

It's important for every affiliate program to offer individual links to specific products.

If a possible buyer lands on a homepage instead of the product sales page, they will most likely move somewhere else. Do you want to lose a sale just because of one small niggle? Most of the affiliate programs have this feature, but in case it's not there, reach out to your affiliate manager and place a request.

Custom link option:

Following up on the point above, pricing pages is not considered a "product page". However, sometimes to **showcase the product** (on a blog or review site), you might *want to link to a pricing page*. Using a direct link, in this case, will be a *big mistake* and will result in you losing out on a lot of potential sales.

How about an option to create a **custom link** for **any page** using your affiliate URL?

This feature is something which the Elegant Themes affiliate program offers (see screenshot below for clarity).

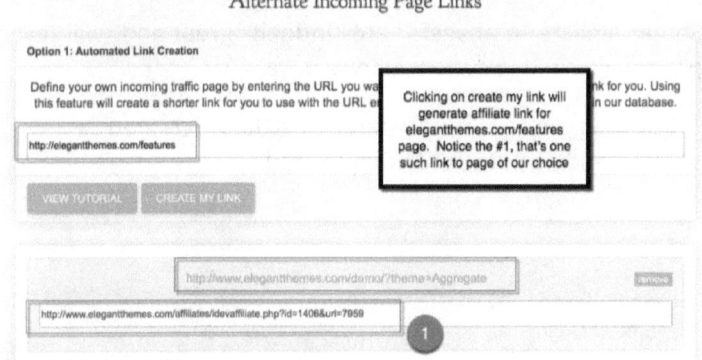

Custom discount coupon code:

Discount coupon codes are **one of the best** methods for promoting *a product*, as it **encourages** sales. Most affiliate programs, especially hosting affiliates, offer discount coupons.

You can always use *their* code, but wouldn't it be better to create your **own branded discount coupon code?**

For example, here's a custom discount coupon code for my HostGator Hosting affiliate account: **SHOUTMELOUD30 (for 30% off).**

This discount code helps me to get about $520/month in extra affiliate sales.

Apart from offering discounts, such coupon codes help in branding. Very few affiliate products provide an option to create custom discount coupons, but it is **incredibly useful** for affiliate marketers like us.

- *Pro Tip:* If you refer more than two sales a month, you should ask your program's affiliate manager to create an exclusive coupon for you.

Some affiliate managers are **indeed great** and will even provide you with a *custom landing page*.

Below is an example where HostGator created a specific landing page for ShoutMeLoud.

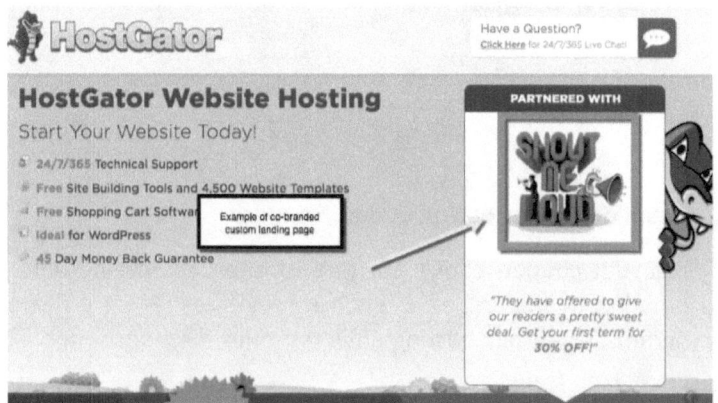

Email updates:

Let us assume you are now a part of one of the top selling products as an affiliate promoter and the company is currently running a **great deal or offer** which nobody can refuse.

But you only got to know about it after ten other bloggers have already written about it, and the promotion is coming to an end.

Make sure you are subscribed to the product affiliate newsletter or ping the affiliate manager to add you to the affiliate email list.

Alternatively, you should also *subscribe to product updates*, FB pages, Twitter pages, or any other ways in which you can stay updated with the latest happenings about the product.

Affiliate stats and banners:

So you just joined an affiliate program.

You log into your affiliate console area and you realize that there is **nothing** apart from your affiliate link and an "edit profile" option.

You can't track how many hits you are sending to them or which page or promotional method is working best for you.

Moreover, there is no offering of any promotional banners or links.

How annoying!

For me, I might refuse to work with such affiliate programs and will find another similar (and equally good) product. *Having a fully-fledged affiliate panel is essential for any successful affiliate program.*

Note: At times when a new product is launched, integrating affiliate programs can be a challenge for companies. They will give you a unique link but can't provide an affiliate dashboard. Sometimes it's OK to make an exception and let the sales flow naturally.

The only thing that I wouldn't do here is pro-actively promote the product. After all, I'm unsure of being paid for my efforts.

How To Select The Best Affiliate Product For Your Blog

To be a successful affiliate marketer, you need to pick and promote the **right product** on your blog.

Over 76% of newbie affiliate marketers fail to earn *any money* from affiliate marketing because they *never pick the right product* to promote.

Tasting success in affiliate marketing is not easy, but it's not as difficult either. You need to be persistent, consistent and have a **proper marketing plan**. If you do these three things, you *will be successful* in the world of affiliate marketing.

Some of the deciding factors are:

- The affiliate products you promote
- The medium you use to promote them
- The efficiency of your sales funnel
- Targeting the right audience
- The plan – is it concrete or is it a 'hit or miss' strategy?

The reason *why I've earned millions* from affiliate marketing is that I only promote products that I have personally tested and used. There was a time when I promoted things without testing them. Those products weren't right and had a negative impact on **my brand**. I was lucky this happened in the initial stages, but I had to learn this lesson the hard way.

As I mentioned earlier, I use the "education method" to make my living online. It's time-consuming, but at the same **it's safe**, and the rewards are *consistent*.

Writing how-to guides and tutorials do help in promotion. It doesn't matter whether you are the *creator or curator* as long as you ensure that your target audience uses *your* affiliate links to purchase a product.

Soon, I will share the tricks that I personally follow to choose **only the best** products to promote.

Before we move ahead, let's take a look at the things we have learned so far:

- **Affiliate marketplace:** This is a marketplace where companies list their product(s), and as an affiliate, you can select which products you want to promote. Here, you will see stats like *overall conversion rate*, *the payout*, and other data-based details that help you pick the best products to endorse.

- **Native/In-house Affiliate program:** Many products have a native affiliate program. Recall the example of TubeBuddy in the first section of this book, which is an example of a **native affiliate program**.

Usually, it's beneficial to join an affiliate program via an *affiliate marketplace,* as their *tracking mechanisms are robust*. You can also easily reach the minimum payout by promoting *multiple products* from the same marketplace.

By using a **quality marketplace**, *you lower down the chances of being cheated*.

START WITH AN AFFILIATE MARKETPLACE

Also, the best place to **start hunting for affiliate products** is in a marketplace (like ShareASale or Commission Junction). Depending on your niche, you can find excellent affiliate products to promote.

Most of these affiliate marketplaces have sections which show their most popular affiliate products.

On the next page, you can see a screenshot from the ShareASale affiliate marketplace, which shows the top 100 hottest selling products:

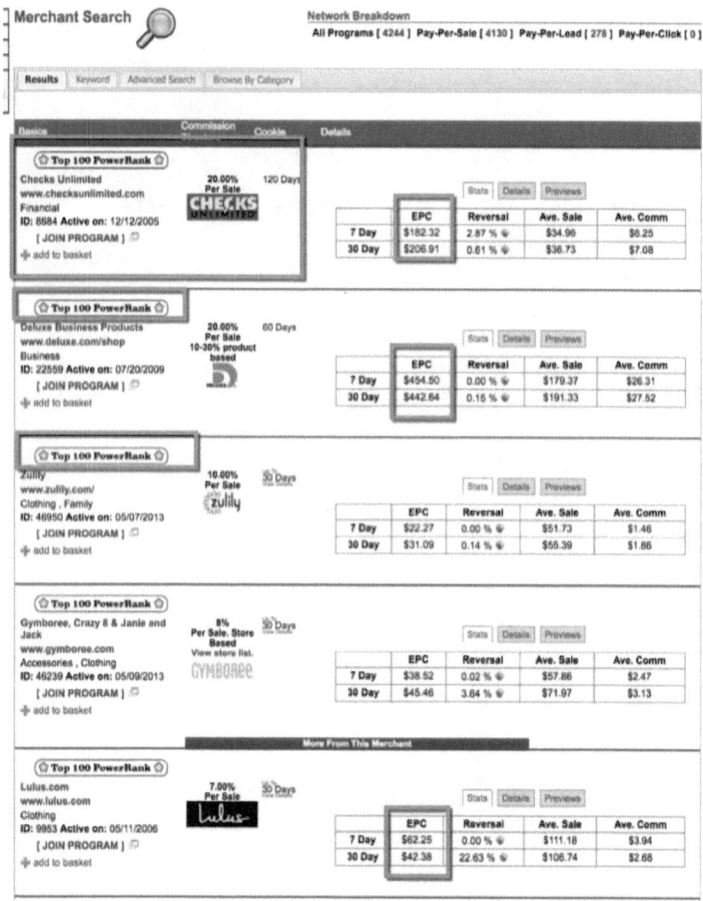

Remember, every marketplace has a *different set of features* and layout structure. Soon, I will be launching a membership site where you can get your hands on *videos for every popular affiliate marketplace*. For now, ShareASale is one affiliate marketplace that you should join ASAP!

THE BENEFITS OF AFFILIATE MARKETPLACES

Affiliate Marketplaces have many benefits. Here's a quick overview.

All the niches in one place:

One of the significant problems we face as an affiliate is finding an affiliate program that aligns with our niche. The advantage of an affiliate marketplace is that you can find **many affiliate programs in various categories**.

Easy to reach minimum payout:

When you sign-up for an affiliate program directly (in-house affiliate program), the biggest challenge is to reach the minimum payout. In an affiliate marketplace, your minimum payout is the **sum of all the affiliate programs** that you promote. For a beginner, it's *much easier* to reach the minimum payout in a marketplace.

Fewer chances of affiliate sale frauds:

In the past, when I joined the affiliate program of a popular online company (HostGator) with their in-house affiliate software, it was a disaster. *I had no choice but to blog about it.*

I wrote a blog post and also made a video on YouTube.

HostGator didn't like it, but eventually, they *understood the problem* and moved their program to ImpactRadius, which offers better tracking.

At times, direct affiliate programs cannot track sales due to improper configurations of their affiliate software, or a new affiliate manager. Sometimes **they simply don't want to pay you**.

With an affiliate marketplace, you don't have to worry about this problem. Their tracking mechanism is **excellent**, and you will be paid for your hard (and not-so-hard) work.

Examples of Affiliate Marketplace: ShareASale, Amazon, Commission Junction, etc.

If a product is not listed in the affiliate marketplace, you can directly search for that particular affiliate program. Let me explain how:

JOIN AFFILIATE PROGRAMS INDIVIDUALLY

Most online products have their **in-house affiliate programs**.

All you need to do is find the hottest selling products in your niche and find the opportunity to market these products.

For example, if you run a blog about dogs, you can try to find an affiliate program related to **dog food** or **dog care**.

To find these companies, you can simply use Google search with the following query:

"site:domain.com affiliate" or "(product name) + affiliate program + Country".

Examples:

- WordPress (Product name) + Affiliate Program
- Fashion (Niche) + Affiliate Program
- Fashion (Niche) + Affiliate Program + Country
- Site:Domain.com + Affiliate

You can see an example of one such Google search in the below screenshot:

These are manual searches, but this works in *most cases*, especially when you are in a **niche** where it is difficult to find an affiliate product in a marketplace.

WHAT IS A "NICHE AFFILIATE" PRODUCT?

You must have noticed that I have used the phrase "niche product" multiple times in this book so far.

A **niche affiliate product** means a product *based* on your blog's topics and your blog's readers. Suppose you run a blog about health (i.e. 'the health niche'); you should be promoting a product *related to health* on your blog.

My advice for you is to **select the best selling products** in your niche and start *writing about them*. It will help you drive traffic and *boost your conversion rates*.

Conversion rates determine the difference between successful and failed affiliate campaigns.

If you get 100 clicks on your affiliate campaign but your conversion rate is a meager 0-1%, you need to re-think your strategy.

One *big* **mistake:**

The most common mistake a newbie affiliate marketer makes is **spending hours** promoting a *low-quality* product. With this approach, a marketer fails before even getting started.

- *Pro Tip: Don't make this mistake!*

What you can do instead is spend *quality time* **learning** about the product.

- Test it out yourself or read reviews by experts or authority bloggers.
- Review the previous products launched by the company.
- Spend time in **finding the right product to promote**.

Don't fall into the trap of marketers who promise tons of money and ultimately pay nothing.

- *Pro Tip:* Sign up for a free-trial of the product if it's available, or ask the product owner to give you a review/sample piece. The latter technique is favorite among fashion and technology/gadget bloggers.

In a worst-case scenario, you can **buy and use the product** to come up with an informed review.

Note: 60% of my affiliate sales come from reviews and tutorials related to the product.

While signing up for *an affiliate program*, you should pay attention to:

- Available banners
- Promotional materials
- Affiliate control panel
- Minimum payout
- Payment method
- Tax form requirements

Things to keep in mind:

- Don't *limit yourself* to a specific network or program
- Some products may not have an affiliate program today, but that doesn't mean they will not have one later. Last year, I used a growth hack method to earn **$1,200 in one month from affiliate marketing**. This trick is perfect for anyone with an existing blog. You can read about it and watch the video here (http://www.shoutmeloud.com/video/growth-hacking-affiliate-earning).

These things will help you decide whether or not you are ready to promote the product.

Suppose you select a seasonal product, and its minimum

payout is $1000. Are you sure you are going to get those many conversions in an off-season?

Bonus Tip: Associating with famous brands will be an added advantage to your affiliate marketing campaign.

Top Affiliate Networks/ Marketplaces

Now that you understand **the features and benefits of joining an affiliate marketplace** let's look at **the best affiliate networks** that you can join today and start making money.

These networks are in order of my personal preferences and the ones that work out the best for me. Some of them may have limited affiliate programs to promote but don't discard any based on **that** criterion alone. The reason being:

- *You only need one great product* to endorse to earn thousands of dollars (if not millions).

ShareASale:

If you have attended an affiliate summit or watched affiliate summit videos, chances are you already know about it. This affiliate network was founded in 2000 and ever since, has paid out **millions of dollars** to their affiliates. They have a great list of affiliate programs for all types of niches.

Even though their interface is not as modern as their competitors, you will have no problem understanding it.

ShareASale makes it easy for you to get started with affiliate marketing. If you want to know how a company offers an affiliate program on ShareASale, you should read their marketing guide. It will give you a kind of "backstage view" of the other side of affiliate marketing.

You can join the ShareASale program now. It usually takes 2-3 working days to get an approval.

Link to join: https://account.shareasale.com/a-login.cfm

CJ.com (Commission Junction):

CJ is one of the **oldest and most popular** affiliate marketplaces out there. You will **find tons of affiliate products** in all niche types. I use (and have been using) CJ for a few selected affiliate programs for many years.

CJ is one marketplace you *must* be on.

Link to join: http://www.cj.com

Amazon's Affiliate Program:

Amazon has an affiliate program that you can join for free.

Since Amazon is a trusted place and has **tons of products** from all niche types, the Amazon affiliate program can help you generate **more than a decent income.**

Link to join: https://affiliate-program.amazon.com/promotion/affiliate-programs.html

Learn how to create affiliate link on Amazon: https://www.shoutmeloud.com/how-to-create-affiliate-link-for-amazon-product-tutorial.html

ClickBank:
ClickBank is another popular marketplace for affiliate marketers. Here, you will find **tons of offers** which you can join and promote.

I will share more about ClickBank in another section.

Join ClickBank: http://affiliatemarketing.buzz/go/Clickbank/

Find affiliate offers using affiliate search engine:

This particular trick will *save you a lot of time*. Also, *very few people know about this*.

Use oDigger or Offervault to find affiliate offers:

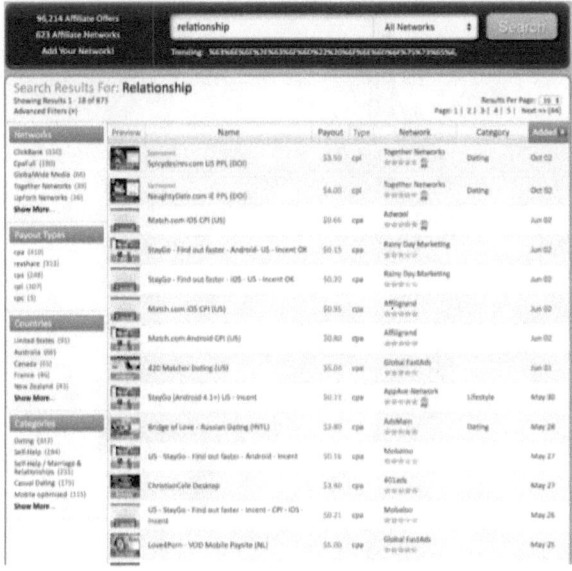

You can use either of these two sites to find affiliate offers in *any niche*. They are like search engines for finding affiliate offers and are *very useful* when you are working on a **new niche** and looking for high converting offers.

Affiliate marketplaces are the **best places to start**. You can browse your niche in these marketplaces and find top performing affiliate programs.

Alternatively, many **niche-based forums** are a *great place* to find new products to promote.

- *Pro Tip:* You should keep an eye on blogs in your niche and check the product(s) they promote and also the methods they use to do so.

Tasks for this section (only for those who currently have a functional blog or a website:

1. Create an account on ShareASale
2. Create an account on CJ.com
3. Create an account on the Amazon affiliate program
4. Create an account on ClickBank

The Art Of Promoting An Affiliate Product On Your Blog

One of these days you're going to have to implement what you have learned and start promoting products.

Now is the perfect time to get into action mode and learn the art of promoting a product on your blog.

Remember, there are other ways of promotions (like PPC marketing, Email marketing, etc.). But for now, we will focus on promoting via blogs. Later, you can use *any other method* to **quadruple** your earnings.

At the end of this chapter, I will share the **one mistake** that *many innocent affiliate marketers make,* and also the *fix* for it.

To start, let's learn the art of affiliate product promotion using your blog.

Review post:

Nothing beats a killer review post about a product to drive conversions via your affiliate link. A review article **introduces the product** to your blog readers. At the same time, your opinion and experience also help them understand why they should buy the product.

There are a few things that you should *always remember* when writing a review post for your affiliate product:

- Reviews should be **honest**. Most of the time, people focus on pros of the product and *ignore the cons*. An honest review should **present both sides of the coin**.

- If you don't like writing, you can always hire a good writer to do the job for you while you take care of other aspects of your online business.

- Don't forget to add product images.

- Write a review in a personal tone (first or second person). You will connect better with your audience. Remember, the person reading the review is *only one person*.

- Again, **pick a product that you use or are likely to use**.

- Take advantage of **star ratings** in search engines to get a higher CTR for your reviews. You can use WP Review pro to add star ratings to your blog posts. Your results in SERPs will look like this:

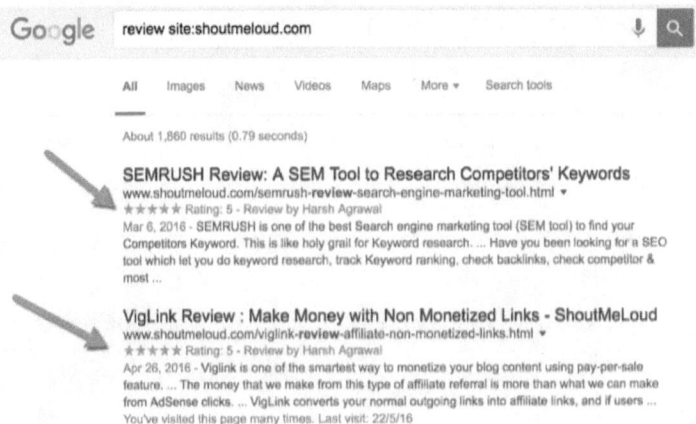

Blog post promotion:

A proper technique is to use affiliate links inside your blog posts and then promote those posts. For this, you should always write *highly targeted posts*.

For example, write an article that a user would search *right before* deciding to buy something. Write posts based on a *buying-intent keyword*.

This will increase your sales by *at least* 200%.

Examples:

- Best [product name] (online)
- Best [product name] site
- Best [product name] website
- Best + product type + in (current year).
- Discount [product name]
- [Product name] coupon
- [Product name] coupon code

- [Product name] discount
- Buy [Product name]
- Buy [Product name] online etc.

Specific post title examples:

- Which GoPro camera model should you buy for shooting underwater?
- How to save money on international flight bookings to Cancun?

Which brings us to....

How-to articles:

A DIY kind of article **always** works well for affiliate product promotion.

If your product is technical or needs instructions before one can use it, you can write a tutorial guide on how to use it properly.

Such tutorials are not only handy but will also help **you improve your search engine rankings**. "How-To" articles *always perform great* on search engines.

Use Coupon Codes:

It's no surprise that people want to save money. Offering your readers the opportunity to save money is **one of the biggest marketing gimmicks ever created**.

Coupons are the next best thing to "free". Whenever customers buy a product and see a coupon box, they search for "Product Name + coupon". I'm sure you've done the same. I do it all the time.

When you offer these coupons, you provide the customer the opportunity to save money while you earn your commission as an affiliate. Win-Win-Win!

Remember, your goal as an affiliate marketer is to **make the customer click on the affiliate link** failing which the sale will not fall in your kitty. Therefore, if you offer a coupon, *make sure users click on your link* to see the coupon code.

If you've ever been on a discount coupon site, you must have seen links where the site asks you to "Click to view coupon" or "Click to go to the merchant site". The reason for this is to make the potential customer drop the cookie with the marketer's affiliate link which will, in turn, help you earn a commission.

Use a WordPress website & trick to increase sales:

When it comes to selecting a blogging platform, you shouldn't look anywhere other than WordPress. WordPress **powers 25% of the websites in the world**.

One of the reasons why WordPress is the preferred choice for creating a blog, a coupon site, or a general website is that it lets you do amazing things with just a few clicks.

As an example, I'm going to share with you **one simple yet powerful trick** to **increase your sales** from *existing* blog posts.

Whether it's a review post or a coupon code post, your first goal is to get more **views on these posts**. Apart from on-page Search Engine Optimization (SEO), you should give more visibility to such affiliate posts by placing it as *a featured post* (the first post on your homepage).

It is a very convenient WordPress feature. You can stick *any post* on your blog's homepage. Here is how to do that:

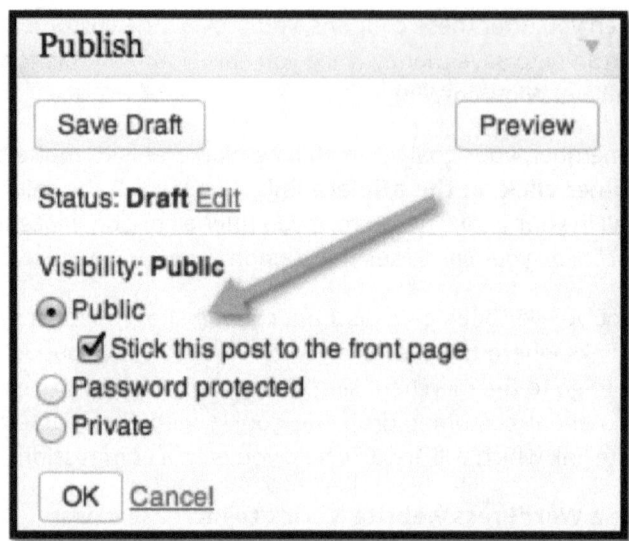

In the *Edit Post* section, click on *Visibility* and put a check mark on "*Stick this post to the front page*".

I have tried this with a few pillar posts on ShoutMeLoud, and it **helped a lot** in increasing my reader base.

Use banners on the sidebar (with a clear call to action):

Banner advertisements work great if you get targeted organic traffic on your blog.

For me, a significant part of my conversions come from banner clicks. A prominent banner placement and technique is the key. One of the **most common mistakes** that people make is they *add too many banners*, and that confuses the visitor.

Rule of thumb:

- **Never place similar products' banners on your sidebar**

- Banner ads work as a **recommended product**, and with *multiple similar products*, you only confuse your readers. A good idea is to place **different related products** in a niche. For example, a WordPress tips blog can place banner ads for a theme, a plugin, and a hosting service together on the same sidebar.

If your blog covers more than one niche, you should consider using the WP Advanced ads plugin for your ad management. The plugin will help you show ads **based on category** and/or **geographical location**. You can also run A/B testing of different banners.

Bonus Tip: When placing ads, link out to the website directly instead of your review post. One big mistake many affiliate marketers make is they try to link an ad to their review post or another internal post. This is wrong because a product landing page is optimized for higher conversion. Though, if the product landing page is not of high quality, you are better off educating users first with your review post.

How Google Treats Affiliate Links For Search Engine Ranking

One of the primary concerns of most affiliate marketers is dealing with **affiliate links from an SEO perspective**.

One significant way to make sure your *affiliate site grows* and **doesn't get penalized** due to affiliate links is by making sure you are *adding value* through your content.

An affiliate site should also be **appropriately promoted and maintained** like any other high-quality site.

To make sure Google doesn't penalize you for using affiliate links, you need to take care of a few things.

As mentioned by Matt Cutts, former head of Google's spam division, in most cases, Google handles affiliate links without any issue, as they know about the majority of affiliate networks. But if you are still worried, you can add a *no-follow link* to your affiliate links.

Now, if you are new to the "no-follow" term, you can learn more about it here:

- http://www.shoutmeloud.com/how-to-add-nofollow-link-attribute-to-any-link-seo.html

HOW TO DEAL WITH AFFILIATE LINKS, SEO IN WORDPRESS:

There are many free and paid affiliate plugins available. I have only played with a few of these WordPress affiliate plugins, but luckily I stumbled upon **one of the best** ones – *ThirstyAffiliates*.

In ThirstyAffiliate's settings, there is an option that lets you add a no-follow attribute to **all links cloaked using this plugin**, which helps you stop passing "link juice" to affiliate links.

Also, I suggest you add the ThirstyAffiliates URL trigger *in your* robots.txt *file as "disallow".*

For example, my URL trigger for affiliate links is */recommended/* and in my WordPress robots.txt file, I have the following lines:

- User-agent: *
- Disallow: /recommended/

This is to make sure Google doesn't crawl such links, and your website is not penalized for any affiliate linking.

This is *only a solution for those who use the ThirstyAffiliates WordPress plugin.* For others, you should start adding the no-follow tag to such links.

For old posts, where you have used direct affiliate links, you can use the Link Status Pro Plugin to add the "no-follow" attribute quickly.

I assume you use plugins like ThirstyAffiliates to mask your affiliate links because default links look ugly and might lower your CTR.

(I have already explained to you the benefits of link cloaking in an earlier section, but it's an important thing to remember.)

How You Can Effectively Increase Affiliate Sales

So how do you feel about these basic promotion tips thus far? Some of the ideas I have shared with you are *trade secrets*, but there are many more which A-list bloggers like Darren Rowse, John Chow, and, at times, Pat Flynn use for promoting a product.

What I'm going to share now will likely **change your outlook towards making money from affiliate marketing**. Instead of looking it as a *quick money making scheme*, you will start seeing it as a way of **"living the life"**.

Don't believe me? Well, how do you think I was able to afford a $300,000 apartment at the age of 29?

Affiliate marketing requires **serious marketing and**

networking skills. One way to earn money is by staying invisible (density-less websites) and driving traffic through PPC, searches, and banners to make sales through non-blogging ways.

Another (and in my opinion, *better*) way is to **create a blog**, share *useful* information, earn people's trust, and give them something that *they can't refuse*.

This sounds simple, but the road to becoming a **six-figure affiliate marketer** is not easy. However, in the process, you will learn many other things which will help make it simpler as you go along.

Here are some tips that you can use *immediately* to help increase your affiliate sales.

Build your reputation: Become an authority

Your **reputation** will be one of the **most useful tools** in your journey of making money online.

It's not very hard to conceptualize. **It's really just common sense**. If your audience trusts you and the material you provide them with, it will be easier for them to believe in the products you're selling or leading them onto.

If you don't want to sell a product *yourself*, you can *lead them to other sites*, and make money by producing those leads.

But, **be aware of how this will impact your reputation**. Always be sure that you're leading your readers to a reliable site.

Tell your audience what to do next:

Remember that your readers are on your site **because of** *your site*, and *not because of the other sites that you are linking to.*

Sometimes, even if you post a link here and there, you'll gain nothing out of them. Your readers will leave, and you won't make money.

To effectively *increase affiliate sales*, you have to *tell your audience what to do next*. An excellent way to drive your readers to an affiliate's site is by slipping in the words "free" and "freebie" into your links.

Everyone (you and I included) loves freebies, and when your readers click on these links, your affiliate commissions **will go through the roof**.

Drive targeted traffic using SEO & PPC:

More traffic on your site will mean a better chance of selling more products with your affiliates.

It's an unsaid rule that if you want to make money online, **you'll have to target people**. You have to build your site around the idea of *attracting your target audience*.

This is done by using keywords, creating quality content, and doing the *right kind of marketing*. This will result in your site being visible on search engines for **relevant keywords.**

Even if you're inexperienced with marketing affiliates, you'll soon find out that **more traffic** will make it easier for you to make **more money** with your links.

I suggest you use WordPress for creating your next affiliate site. When you do, you can refer to this **big list** of the best WordPress plugins for SEO (https://www.shoutmeloud.com/best-recommended-seo-wordpress-plugins.html) and optimize your site for better search engine ranking.

Base your actions on conversion:

When marketing affiliates, you will **always have to upgrade** consistently. You will need to base these actions on conversion rates.

Suppose you have 300 visitors a day and only three of them click on your link or product. That subtly means you need to change the way you market. Think from the customer's point of view.

Ask these questions to yourself:

- Does anything on your site make people **want to click** on a link or product? Branch off ideas from that.
- Does anything on your site make people **not want** to buy the linked product? Remove and avoid these.

These are some of the necessary steps that you can follow, but I suggest you conduct **proper research** about the product(s) that you are promoting. Promoting a hot, trending, and popular product is usually a "go" for **viral promotion.**

Marketing affiliates is all about **business strategy** and **engaging with your audience.** If you want to **increase affiliate sales**, you need to lead your audience to something that they will appreciate.

How To Start Using ShareASale Affiliate Marketplace & Make Money

In this section, you will learn everything about ShareASale.

In the next 15 minutes, you will be **all set to start earning** from this popular affiliate marketplace.

WHAT IS SHAREASALE & HOW DOES IT WORK?

ShareASale, a popular service for marketers to launch an affiliate program for their product or services, came into existence in the year 2000. On ShareASale, bloggers and affiliate marketers can find and join affiliate programs.

Marketers who plan to launch an affiliate program, can join ShareASale and use their *welcome kit* and *training webinars* to educate themselves.

Before I share the guide, you should know these four terms (many of which we've already covered):

- **Merchants:** Merchants are *business owners* who set up an affiliate program so that affiliates can join and drive more sales to their business in return for a fixed commission.

- **Affiliate Marketers:** Users like you and me who join an affiliate program and promote it via a blog, PPC, or other methods.

- **Affiliate Software:** This could be self-hosted or a service like ShareASale, ClickBank, or CJ where an affiliate program is hosted. In this case, ShareASale is the affiliate software.

- **Affiliate Marketplace:** A marketplace where an affiliate can discover new opportunities and join an affiliate program. At the same time, businesses get to expose their affiliate program to affiliate marketers.

Now that you have a clear understanding of the basic terminology let's understand how to use ShareASale's affiliate marketplace.

- **Step 1: Head over to ShareASale &** signup for a free account (http://www.shoutmeloud.com/recommended/Shareasale).

- Click "Move On To Step 2".

To create an affiliate account on ShareASale, you **need to have a website**. Even if you plan to promote an affiliate deal using PPC, Google AdSense, or any other means, you **still need to have a site**.

If you don't have one at this moment, you can follow this guide (http://www.shoutmeloud.com/how-to-install-wordpress-and-steps-after-installing-wordpress.html) and set up your website in the next 25 minutes.

- Fill out the information:

PRIMARY AFFILIATE WEBSITE

- PRIMARY WEBSITE ASSOCIATED WITH ACCOUNT
- OTHER WEBSITES MAY BE ADDED TO THE ACCOUNT LATER
- THIS WEBSITE WILL BE VISIBLE TO MERCHANTS WHEN APPLYING TO THEIR PROGRAMS
- THIS WEBSITE WILL BE USED TO VERIFY INFORMATION YOU ENTER.

IMPORTANT: YOU MUST HAVE AND OPERATE AT LEAST ONE WEBSITE IN ORDER TO CREATE AN AFFILIATE ACCOUNT AT SHAREASALE.COM. IF YOU PLAN ON DOING MOST OF YOUR ADVERTISING AND PROMOTION USING PAY PER CLICK, GOOGLE ADSENSE, OVERTURE, ETC..., YOU STILL MUST HAVE A WEBSITE THAT IDENTIFIES YOUR BUSINESS.

HTTP:// shoutmeloud.com

WEBSITE INFORMATION

PLEASE ANWSER THE YES/NO QUESTIONS BELOW AND CHECK ANY BOXES THAT PERTAIN TO THE WEBSITE ABOVE. IMPORTANT: PROVIDING DETAILS ABOUT YOUR WEBSITE WILL SPEED UP YOUR APPLICATION APPROVAL.

YOUR WEBSITE IS WRITTEN IN WHAT LANGUAGE?
English

DOES YOUR WEBSITE CONTAIN ADULT CONTENT OR LINK TO SITES THAT CONTAIN ADULT CONTENT?
○ YES ● NO

DO YOU UTILIZE SPONSORED LISTINGS IN PAY PER CLICK SEARCH ENGINES AS PART OF YOUR PROMOTIONAL STRATEGY? YES ○ NO ○
DO YOU UTILIZE COUPONS AS PART OF YOUR PROMOTIONAL STRATEGY? YES ● NO ○
DO YOU UTILIZE A BROWSER "ADD ON", TOOLBAR, OR OTHER DOWNLOADABLE APPLICATION AS PART OF YOUR PROMOTIONAL STRATEGY? YES ○ NO ●
ARE YOU AN ADVERTISING NETWORK OR AFFILIATE NETWORK? YES ○ NO ●
DO YOU HAVE A NETWORK OF PUBLISHERS TO WHICH YOU DELIVER ADS? YES ○ NO ●
DO YOU DISPLAY ADVERTISEMENTS ON SITES THAT YOU DON'T OWN? YES ○ NO ●

MOVE ON TO STEP 3

Note: *When you join with a merchant, they will see your primary website. If you enter any non-working webpage, chances are your application will be rejected.*

- **Enter your email address in Step 3.**
- The last step is to enter your details like *name, address & payment details*. Don't worry about payment as

ShareASale offers payment via check, ACH, and others methods which you can configure later.

CONTACT INFORMATION

We need to get some contact information from you so that we are able to send your payments. Please note that ShareASale.com does not, in any circumstance, give away or sell your contact information to ANY other company.

FIRST NAME:	Harsh
LAST NAME:	Agrawal
MAKE CHECKS PAYABLE TO:	Harsh Agrawal
CONTACT PHONE:	74936437826
ADDRESS:	Kaveri
ADDRESS 2:	Haug Khas
CITY:	Delhi
STATE / PROVINCE:	New Delhi
ZIP OR POSTAL CODE:	110016
COUNTRY:	India
SUPPORT PHONE PIN:	8080 MUST BE 4 DIGIT NUMBER
DESCRIPTION:	Please provide a brief Description (less than 240 characters) of your site or your marketing plans. You don't need to go into detail about specifics, but anything that you can describe about what you do will help individual merchants make decisions about applications to their programs.

My Site is a high quality content site which gets 90% of the traffic from search engine.

88 / 240

INCENTIVE WEBSITE?

An incentive program is a website that rewards visitors for performing actions. Examples include Pay-To-Read Email sites, Reward or Charity sites, etc...

Please choose one of the following:

○ My site operates as an incentive program.
○ My site is NOT an incentive program.
● I don't know what an incentive program is.

Once done, click "Move To Next Step". This is where you can configure your payment settings (or skip it for now). *Inside your ShareASale dashboard, you can edit or configure your payment settings later.*

Once done, open your email account and click on the confirmation link.

Once all the steps are taken care of, it takes **a day or two to get the approval** of your application.

You can come back here once your application is approved.

I have also made a video tutorial on how to use ShareASale on pro.shoutmeloud.com

Here you will learn:

- How to use the ShareASale dashboard
- How to find top performing affiliate programs on ShareASale
- How to join an affiliate program via ShareASale
- How to configure your payment settings
- How to get links to any affiliate program

How To Using The Amazon Affiliate Program & Start Making Money

In the previous chapter, we discussed how to earn money from the ShareASale marketplace. In this chapter, we will talk about the Amazon affiliate program.

Amazon is one of the world's biggest marketplaces. Even though there are many affiliate marketplaces in the world, many bloggers and big companies use Amazon to sell their products.

Their affiliate program pays you up to 15% of the sale amount and, depending on what kind of sale you are making it's an excellent way to make big money.

This is especially true if you are a gadget or mobile blogger. You can write a complete review of a mobile phone and provide an Amazon affiliate link. By spending 15 minutes of your time and finding the best mobile deal, you can add substantial extra income.

HOW TO SIGN UP FOR AMAZON AFFILIATE PROGRAM?

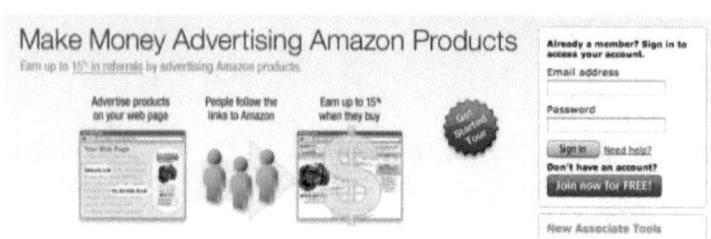

You should sign up for the Amazon affiliate program depending on your geographical location or your target market.

For example, if your target audience is in the United States, you should sign up for Amazon US associate program using this link. If your target audience is from India, you should sign up for the Amazon India program. If you plan to promote products from all Amazon geographical locations, you should sign up for Amazon affiliate program for all countries like .jp (Japan), .au (Amazon Australia) & so on.

Sign Up for Amazon Affiliate program: https://affiliate-program.amazon.com (for Amazon US Store)

For other countries:

- **Canada:** https://associates.amazon.ca
- **United Kingdom:** https://associates.amazon.co.uk
- **Germany:** https://associates.amazon.de
- **France:** https://associates.amazon.fr
- **Japan:** https://associates.amazon.co.jp
- **India:** https://associates.amazon.in
- **Mexico:** https://afiliados.amazon.com.mx

- Brazil: https://associados.amazon.com.br

HOW TO CREATE AFFILIATE LINKS AS AN AMAZON AFFILIATE?

I assume by now you have signed up for the Amazon Associates program.

The next step is to get links, banners, or widgets for your site. Depending on your niche, you can select different types of links. For example:

If you have a gadget blog, you can create a page called "Recommended Gadgets".

If you have a movie or music blog, you can add a widget on the sidebar with the movie's DVD affiliate link.

The possibilities are enormous and, depending on your niche, you can add links and monetize your site to a considerable degree using Amazon.

You will earn money from Amazon affiliate online when someone follows your Amazon referral link and buys something. That also includes further purchases.

Or, just browse the Amazon site while logging into your Amazon affiliate link. On every page at the top, you can find Amazon affiliate link generator which will let you grab Amazon affiliate links instantly.

STEP BY STEP GUIDE TO CREATING AMAZON AFFILIATE LINK

Once your application is approved, log in to your Amazon affiliate panel and head to any product page on the Amazon website. At the top, you will see the option – *Amazon Associates SiteStripe*.

Here, click on Get link > Text

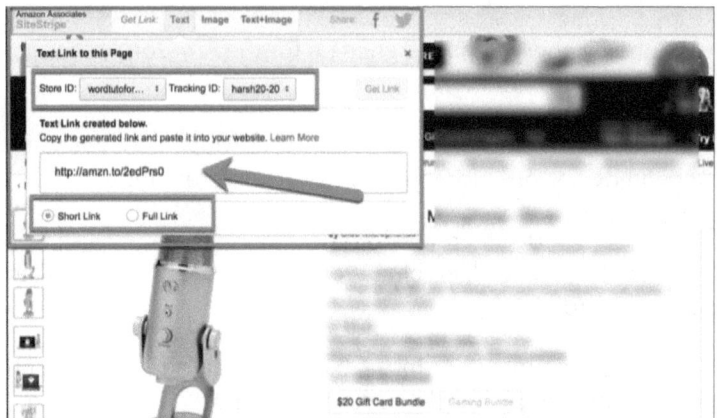

In the above screenshot, you can see how to get your affiliate link. If you use a store ID or tracking ID for tracking purposes, you can change that too. (Don't worry if you haven't started using store ID or tracking ID. We will cover this in the upcoming chapter.)

In case you want to make any changes in theSiteStripe option, you can do so from your Amazon associate account. Here is the direct link (https://affiliate-program.amazon.com/home/account/sitestripe) for making changes in the SiteStripe option.

Another way to create an affiliate link for Amazon products:

The first option is the neatest and fastest, but there are other ways to create an affiliate link for Amazon product too.

Log in to your Amazon associate account and click on Product linking > Product links:

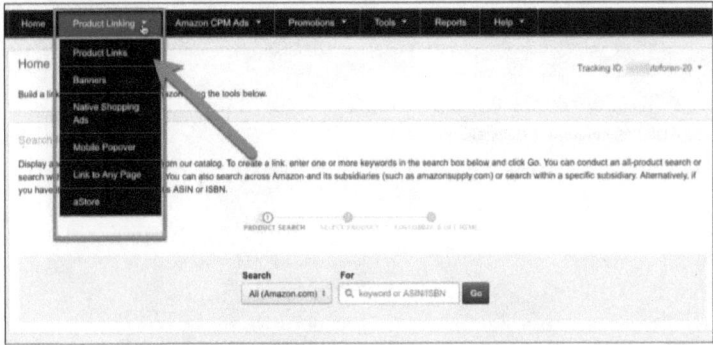

On the next page, you will find two options. Search for a product or add ASIN/ISBN Code of an individual product. I prefer the latter as it's fast. You can find more information about ASIN/ISBN codes at http://www.amazon.com/gp/seller/asin-upc-isbn-info.html .

How to Get ASIN code of individual Amazon product?

The first step is to find the product which is relevant to your website/blog. You can search for any product by going directly to Amazon.com homepage. Once you have found the product, go to *product detail*. In this case, I have the ASIN code of this product.

> **Blue Yeti USB Microphone - Silver**
> $128.99 + $51.75 Shipping & Import Fees Deposit to India Details ▾   In Stock. Ships from and so
>
> **Product Information**
> style:**USB Microphone** | Color:**Silver**
>
> | | |
> |---|---|
> | Item Weight | 4.4 pounds |
> | Product Dimensions | 5 x 5.5 x 10 inches |
> | Shipping Weight | 3.8 pounds (View shipping rates and policies) |
> | Domestic Shipping | This item is also available for shipping to select countries outside the U... |
> | International Shipping | This item can be shipped to select countries outside the U.S. Learn More |
> | **ASIN** | **B002VA464S** |
> | Item model number | YETI |
> | Customer Reviews | ★★★★☆ ▾   4,305 customer reviews
4.5 out of 5 stars |
> | Best Sellers Rank | #126 in Musical Instruments (See Top 100 in Musical Instruments)
#2 in Musical Instruments > Live Sound & Stage > Microphones > Dynamic Microphones > Multipurpose |

Grab the Amazon Affiliate link for the product:

Now we have the ASIN code of the product. Go to Add a Product link page. (Refer Image 1). Add ASIN code of the product and click on the go. Refer to the following image:

Click on get links, and you will be able to get text links or image links that you can paste into your website.

To become an affiliate for Amazon, sign up using this link: https://affiliate-program.amazon.com

HOW TO USE GENI.US TO MAKE MORE MONEY FROM THE AMAZON AFFILIATE PROGRAM

Many of the existing Amazon affiliate partners don't know about *one important thing:*

- Amazon doesn't pay you for sales made in stores in a different country other than the one you have signed up for.

Call it **intelligent links, link localization, global linking, universal linking, or link globalization,** it all means the same thing with regards to the Amazon ecosystem.

The concept of Geni.us is brilliant for any internet marketer, and I like the way they've made it easy for anyone to get started. The onboarding is simple, and once you have created a trial account, you can straight away track how effective this service is going to be for you.

Sign up for Geni.us :https://www.shoutmeloud.com/ recommended/Geni.us/

After you have signed up, you need to copy/paste your Amazon affiliate link to let Geni.us auto-detect the country you are signed up for in the Amazon affiliate program.

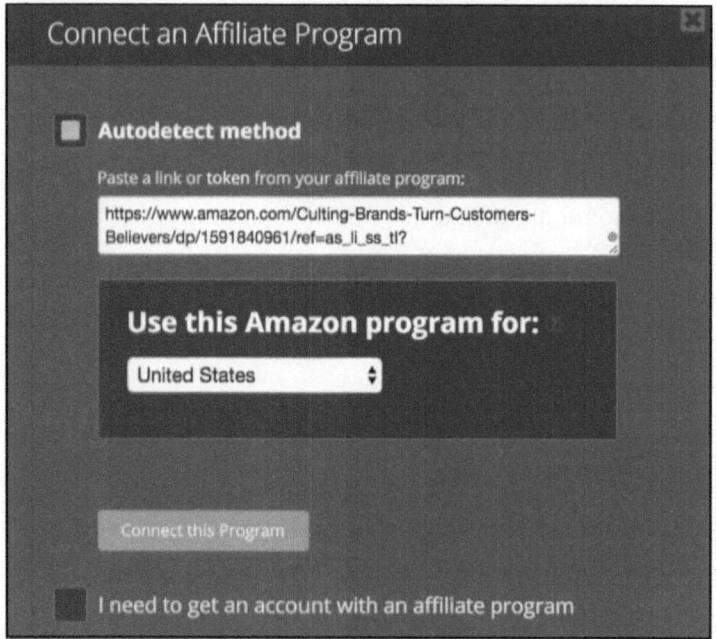

Note: Copy your affiliate URL from the address bar and paste it as shown in the screenshot above. It will auto detect the location, but do cross-check before clicking on "Connect this Program".

This is how it looks for me:

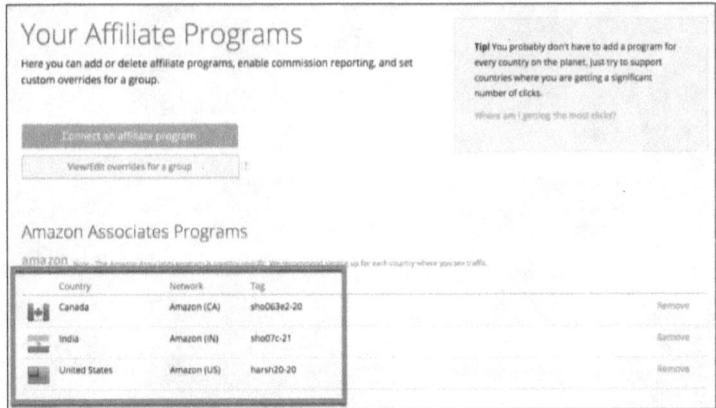

Adding iTunes Affiliate Program

To connect your iTunes affiliate program with Geni.us, you need to copy/paste the token from your PHG account:

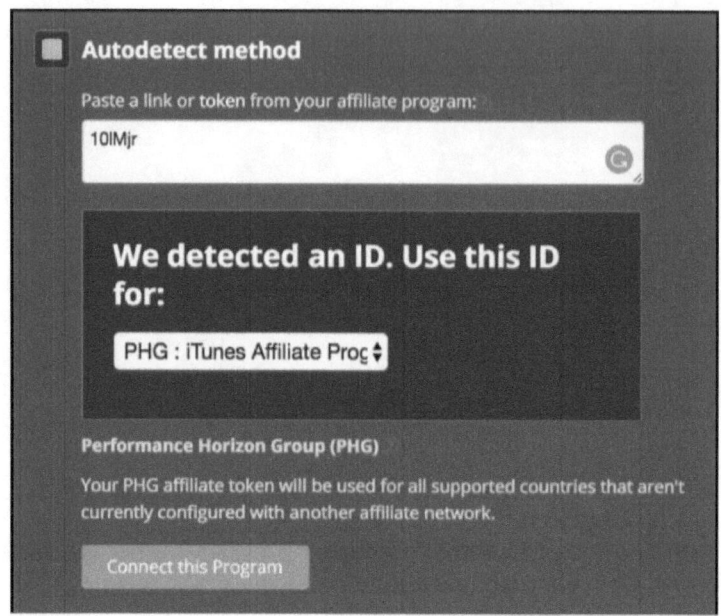

Creating Your First Link

Click on the **"Links"** tab and paste your first affiliate link.

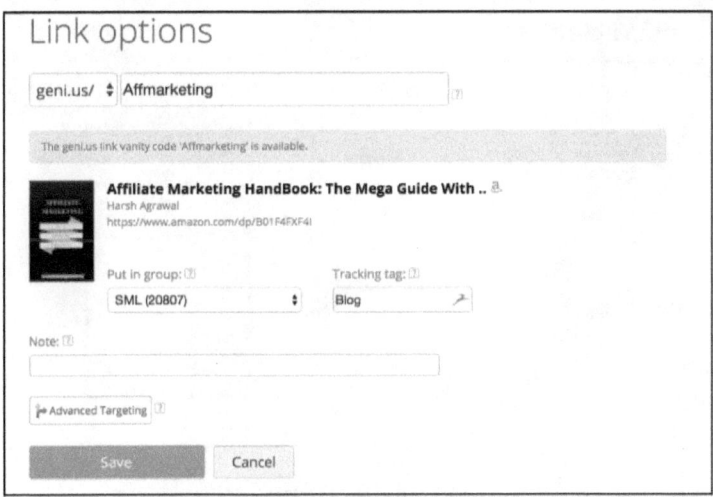

You can learn how to create global Amazon affiliate links here (http://blog.geni.us/2016/03/30/create-global-amazon-product-links/).

Integrating Geni.us with Your Website

The best part is, they offer multiple ways to integrate Geni.us on your website.

Javascript method:

This is the easiest method that works for every platform including BlogSpot. All you need to do is add the lines of code just before the closing </body> or </head> tag. You can use the Google Tag Manager to manage all such tags from one place.

If you have multiple websites, take advantage of the "Group" feature.

WordPress Plugin (Amazon Link Engine):

If you are a WordPress blogger like me, you can use the official Geni.us Amazon link plugin. All you need to do is create an API key from your Geni.us account and configure the WordPress plugin with your API key.

After this, all existing links will automatically be redirected to the affiliate program.

Download the Geni.us Amazon WordPress plugin : https://wordpress.org/plugins/amazon-link-engine/

Note: They also have an iTunes Engine plugin which is for the iTunes affiliate program. Learn about the iTunes affiliate program on this link (http://www.shoutmeloud.com/itunes-affiliate-program.html).

Chrome Add-on

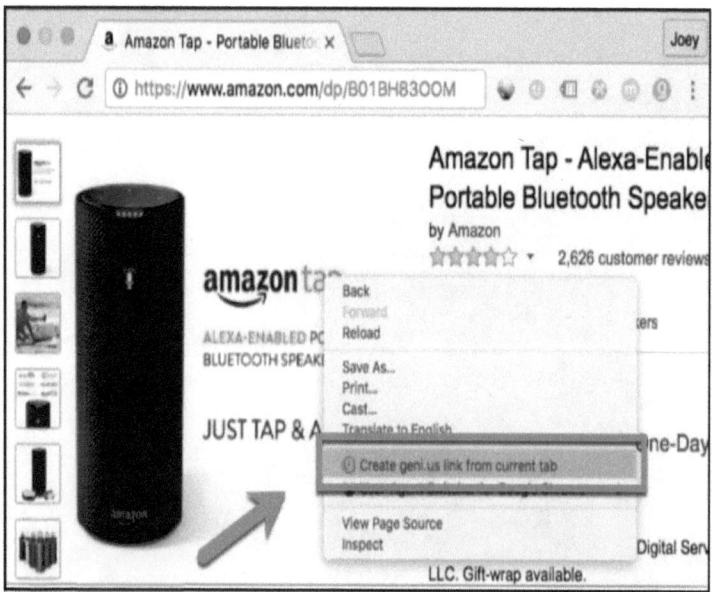

They also have a Chrome add-on which lets you create the

Geni.us link directly from the product page. This is useful when you don't want to use Javascript or the WordPress plugin.

My Amazon income stats after using Geni.us for 30 days:

Before using Geni.us, I was only linking to the Amazon.com store. Once I integrated Geni.us, I started sending traffic to all the Amazon stores based on a user's geo-location. In the graph below, you can see the distribution based on click destination.

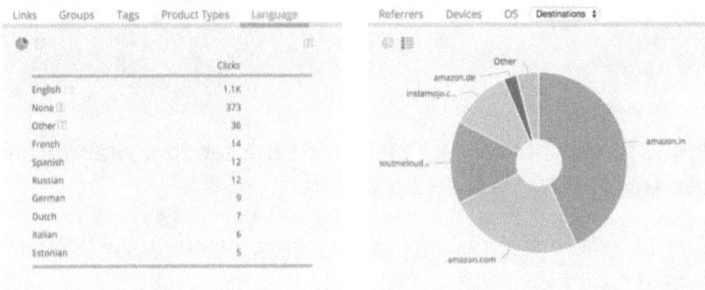

Here are the stats from my Amazon India Associates program which was generating low figures before using Geni.us:

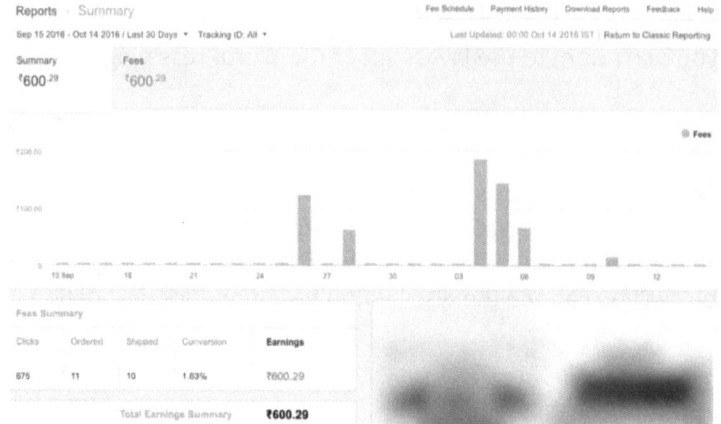

In the screenshot below, you can see the earnings report from the Amazon UK Associates program.

Note: Ignore the amounts as we only promote a few products from Amazon.

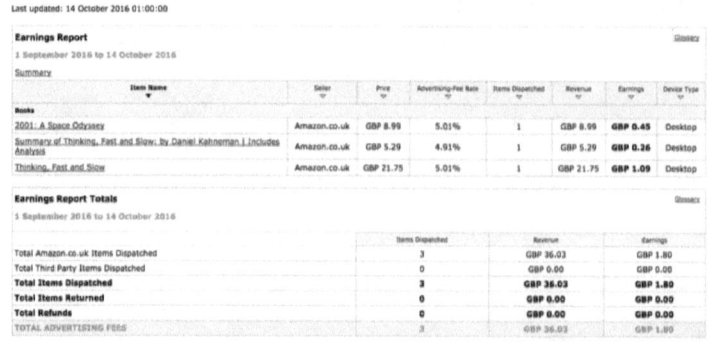

Geni.us pricing:

The pricing of Geni.us is pretty simple as you only need to pay a monthly fee based on the number of clicks.

You can also try it for free with *unlimited clicks for 14 days* which is good enough for you to test out the service.

Take your 14-day free trial :http://www.shoutmeloud.com/recommended/Geni.us/

Well, Geni.is is indeed one tool that every Amazon affiliate should use. Apart from affiliate marketing, you can also use it for various other purposes. For example, you can use it to send users to different pages based on their device or geo-location.

The practical implementations are numerous and I'm pretty sure you will figure out a smart way to use this tool.

Alternative to Geni.us for Amazon Associates: There is a WordPress plugin called *Easy Azon* which is not as powerful as Geni.us, yet popular among marketers who are into the Amazon affiliate niche.

Other Affiliate Marketplaces

ClickBank:

ClickBank is one of the **most popular affiliate marketplaces** out there and a big hub for affiliate marketers. Joining ClickBank is easy, and once you are signed up, you will get your ClickBank username (mine is "denharsh").

ClickBank manages most of the premium WordPress affiliate program plugins. You just need to get the "hop link".

Here is a quick example:

The Instabuilder plugin is managed by ClickBank (CB), and on their affiliate page, you will see a link like:

- *http://clickbankusername.stheresia.hop.clickbank.net*

Simply replace, *"clickbankusername"* with your username (e.g. denharsh), and your affiliate link will become:

- *http://denharsh.stheresia.hop.clickbank.net*

This is going to be the same for all of the themes and plugins that are managed by ClickBank.

Join ClickBank: http://www.shoutmeloud.com/recommended/Clickbank/

JVZoo:

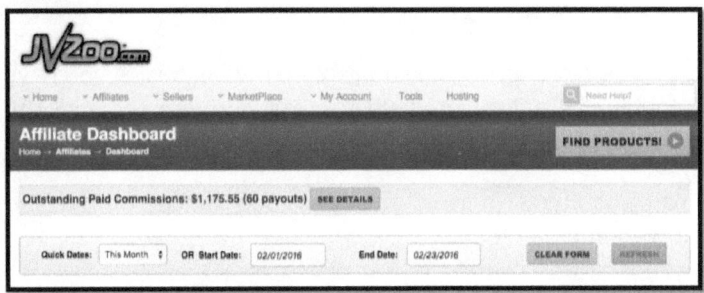

JVZoo is another affiliate marketplace widely used by internet marketers. You will find some fantastic WordPress products out there (plugins and themes), which you can **easily promote**.

Most of these products are *launched by internet marketers,* who know what us bloggers require.

This means that the products are usually very useful.

Joining their program is easy and free.

- Payout via PayPal
- Lifetime cookies

Join JVZoo affiliate program:http://www.shoutmeloud.com/recommended/JvZoo/

Affiliate or AdSense: Which is Better?

So far you have learned the affiliate marketing basics, you have a glossary of affiliate marketing terms, and you know all **the essential elements** of an affiliate program.

You also know where to go to get good affiliate products to promote and market.

Now, if you are an experienced blogger who is *already monetizing* the blog with AdSense, you may be asking this question:

Should I continue using AdSense or remove it altogether?

There's no right or wrong answer here. But there are a few important things to note.

Affiliate marketing is **more rewarding than AdSense** in terms of *revenue* and *not loading up your site with un-moderated ads*.

Affiliate marketing, however, requires **more effort**.

With AdSense, you **just place a code,** and all money making from the blog is on auto-pilot. With blog-based affiliate marketing, **you need to churn out high-quality content on a regular basis along with continually working on finding quality products within a reputable affiliate program**.

Since you have purchased this book, I'm assuming you are not lazy. But, if any of your friends are, you can tell them about Viglinks *&* Skimlinks. *These are like* Infolinks *(in-text ads) and may help generate more money than AdSense.*

By not using Google AdSense, one can easily **clean the clutter** from a blog and make content more concise and readable. At the same time, by using affiliate marketing, you end up **earning more** while *keeping your readers happy*.

Now, let's have a detailed look at some of the **reasons** why affiliate marketing is *better* than AdSense.

On ShoutMeLoud.com, I don't use **any AdSense ads**, but on a few of my blogs such as *LetsTalkRelations.com*, I use *AdSense AND affiliate products*.

In my opinion, AdSense is useful only when you are running a multi-niche blog. But if there is a relevant product to your niche blog, affiliate marketing turns out way more profitable.

Now, about my model:

I use **affiliate marketing banners + AdSense + direct advertisements** to monetize most of my blogs.

People have a misconception that Google is against affiliate marketing. It is *not true*.

Google says **it's perfectly fine** to keep the affiliate links, but it's essential to maintain the **quality of the blog**. If you write shoddy content and put 20 affiliate links in one article, it is bound to affect your website's search engine ranking.

Things to know – AdSense vs. Affiliate Marketing:

- It's **easier** to get into an affiliate network than AdSense.

- Affiliate marketing **pays higher** than AdSense.

- Most affiliate companies offer PayPal as payment method, AdSense doesn't.

- You can find affiliate products for all niches, but AdSense is not allowed on certain niches.

- AdSense gives **recurring income** while *many* affiliates only pay once.

- Affiliate ads are **more attractive** than AdSense ads, but there is no personal control over ads shown by AdSense.

It's quite evident from the points above that affiliate marketing is **more lucrative and beneficial than AdSense**.

But I would suggest you experiment *with both*.

With one affiliate sale, you could be making somewhere between $10-$300 depending on the product that you are promoting.

In my case, *I can make a lot more money* with affiliate marketing than with AdSense.

My experiment of replacing AdSense ads with Affiliate Marketing:

When I wanted to move away from AdSense, it was scary. I wanted to replace it with affiliate banners, but at the same time, I didn't want to lose my monthly recurring income from AdSense.

Finally, I took a leap of faith and did what I **should have done much earlier**.

I took away all prominent AdSense ad spots above my posts and replaced them with a banner for a product that I'm affiliated with.

Do you want to know the result of this experiment?

- *6 sales in 25 days* which resulted in (6*100) $600

I was only making *$280/month* with AdSense.

But let me tell you the **most important thing**. I'm not saying that you should not use AdSense. I'm saying you should *decide your blog monetization methods based on your niche and audience*.

Here at ShoutMeLoud, I have a smart audience that understands the internet and knows what to click and what not to.

On ShoutMeTech.com, a site targeted at tech-enthusiasts who want to read about the latest gadgets, the audience doesn't mind seeing ad banners that are offered by AdSense, Media.net and similar advertising platforms. They don't care about internet marketing as we do.

In simple words, *affiliate marketing works best when you have a niche website with a targeted audience.*

Can you have Amazon Affiliate ads and AdSense on the same page?

Here, I'm using the example of the Amazon affiliate program, but this is **true for all other affiliate programs**. Amazon Associates happens to be one of the most popular affiliate programs. But you can replace Amazon with any other affiliate program.

Newbies tend to worry about using affiliate links on the same page where they are showing AdSense ads.

They fear this might get their account banned.

Well, let's find out how true this is:

The short answer is, **"Yes, you can place affiliate ads along with AdSense ads on the same page, and this doesn't violate AdSense policies."** Here is a screenshot from the official AdSense help page, which clearly says: *"We do allow affiliate or limited-text links."*

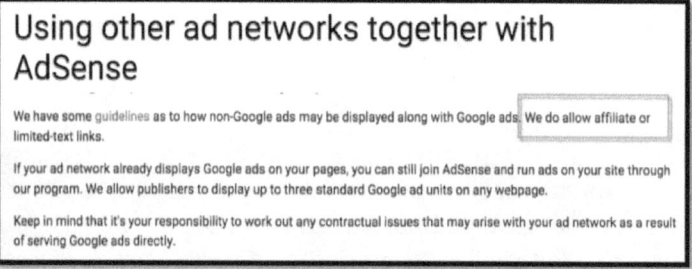

To add more to it, here is an excerpt from the official AdSense help page:

(Note: Affiliate ads are called "different advertising networks" here.)

> **Google ads on the same page with other ads**
>
> You're welcome to display Google ads on the same site or page as other third party advertisements provided that the formatting or colors of the third party ads is different enough from that of the Google ads. In other words, if you choose to place non-Google ads on the same site or page as Google ads, it should always be clear to the user that the ads are served by different advertising networks and that the non-Google ads have no association with Google. If the formats are naturally similar, we ask that you choose different color schemes for the competing ads.
>
> Our intent with this policy is to be as fair to our advertisers as possible and to maintain the integrity of the AdWords and AdSense programs. You can learn more about this, and all our policies, on our program policies page. Please also be aware that competitor ads are considered to be part of your site's content and must follow our policy guidelines.

Before you jump with joy and start adding tons of affiliate banner ads and link ads on your blog, here are a few critical things that you should keep in mind:

- If the number of ads or affiliate banners/links **is more than the original content**, it will put your AdSense account in danger. *Limit the number of ads on your blog*, and focus on **adding value and quality** to your website. I suggest you keep an "optimum limit" of ads that you place on your blog and place them in a way that doesn't hamper user-experience.

- Your affiliate ads should **not link to content which is not allowed** in AdSense's TOS (for example, adult content). AdSense treats other ads (ads from other ad networks or affiliate ads) on a page as *part of the content* and *all* of that content should follow their content guidelines.

- While using affiliate links on your blog, make sure they are "no-follow". **This has nothing to do with AdSense**, but using the no-follow tag is a good practice from an SEO point of view (and is also recommended by Google).

Affiliate or AdSense: Which is Better? | 83

To sum it up...

Yes, you can use affiliate ads with Google AdSense on your website.

But I would recommend you start using affiliate marketing **in addition** to AdSense.

If you have an existing blog, replacing **one of your low performing ad units** with *direct affiliate ads* of a product related to your niche is a good idea.

Once you start garnering success in the form of affiliate sales, replace more AdSense ad blocks with affiliate ads. If you select the *right product to promote*, you can comfortably earn (at a *minimum*) **2-3x of your AdSense earnings** with affiliate marketing.

Note: Amazon has just launched Native Shopping Ads (which is compatible with AdSense).

CPA vs. Affiliate Marketing: A Beginner's Guide To CPA Marketing

CPA is considered to be **easier** than affiliate marketing for one simple reason:

- You get paid for **sending** a lead.

Once the traffic you send converts into a lead, it becomes the job of the particular network to convert that lead into a sale. Irrespective of whether or not that sale gets made, you will **be paid for the lead**.

In CPA, you get paid for sending users who complete an action that could be as simple as getting a user to fill out a form or take any other desired action.

In affiliate marketing, you get paid *only* when a sale goes through.

In short, it's much easier to get a user to do something that doesn't cost money.

How's it different from affiliate marketing?

Here are some more differences between CPA & affiliate marketing:

- You get **paid faster** in a CPA network.
- You are usually on your own in a CPA network. In an affiliate network, you are *assigned an affiliate manager* who keeps you updated on the best offers and shares ways to help you make more money.
- Once you are part of an affiliate network like ShareASale, ClickBank, or any other, you can quickly get affiliate links and start promoting. With CPA, it takes a **much longer** to become part of a network, and **you need to get approval** for the CPA offer that you wish to promote.

Here is a screenshot of my Peerfly dashboard (a popular CPA Network):

FAQ about CPA:

Should you use CPA or affiliate marketing?

One benefit of CPA is it usually converts well (because no direct sale needs to be made) and you can drive traffic from various sources.

At the same time, the downside of CPA in comparison to affiliate marketing is that (because no direct sale is being made) **it pays less**.

The thumb rule to making online income is:

- Don't *limit yourself* to one form of making money online.

For a beginner, it's good to start with CPA as you might not have a blog or a consistent source of traffic.

With CPA, you can see **immediate results** as you will start seeing a few cents in your account when users take simple actions like submitting their email into a form.

How much money can one earn with CPA?

Some people are *making millions* with CPA marketing.

But in terms of single conversions, it could be as low as $0.10 and as high as $10. In some cases where the user **enters their credit card** details for a trial of a product, you can get paid **up to $50**.

How about traffic generation methods?

In CPA, you need to check the details before starting the promotion. Many CPA offers are **limited to specific geographical locations**, and sometimes you can use only *selected sources* to drive traffic.

Below, you can see a screenshot of one offer where the only allowed country is France, and there are specific traffic generation methods.

(Again, taken from the Peerfly CPA network)

> **Conversion Point:** Lead converts on DOI (Double Opt In) completed registration plus email confirmation by a male user.
> **Categories:** Dating
> **Date Added:** Jun 14, 2013
> **Payment Schedule:** Net30 (default)
>
> ✔ **Allowed Methods:** Social PPC, Banner Display, PPV/CPV, Contextual
> ⊘ **Allowed Countries:** France
>
> ⊘ **Not Allowed:** NO Incent, NO Classified Ads, NO Twitter, NO SMS, NO Email Marketing, NO Search PPC, LIMITED Facebook Promotion
>
> Please read this blog post if you do not understand the above terms.

How about the reversal and holding periods for commission payouts?

In affiliate marketing, we have a **holding period of 30-60 days** compared to CPA where you get **paid instantly** with *no refunds* unless you violate the TOS such as driving traffic using an illegal method.

You will be paid **once you reach the minimum payout** for the CPA network you are signed up with.

What about scam offers?

This is one of the *biggest downsides of CPA*.

You will find **a lot of scam offers** paying $1-$2 for simple tasks.

Like this one, where you need to drive traffic to a "win an iPhone/iPad" page:

But I'm sure you are smart enough to know such offers are scams and something you don't want people to fall for. **Avoid offers such as "make money quickly", online flash games (many of them install spyware), sex or dating sites, and others that seem sketchy.**

Use your own judgment and avoid promoting something that looks suspicious or might hurt somebody.

In my opinion, **both affiliate marketing and CPA** are *excellent sources* of earning.

Affiliate marketing is the **slow process**, but with the right strategy, it offers a **much larger payout** in the long run.

At the same time, CPA **is easy for beginners** without a website as you only need to send traffic to take simple actions like email signups or installing an app or completing a survey.

Best Recurring Affiliate Programs

One of the **highly profitable moments** of affiliate marketing is when you find an affiliate that offers recurring income.

I'm assuming by now you are aware of how affiliate marketing works. Basically, you get paid when somebody buys a product using your affiliate link.

But one thing to keep in mind is, there are *many affiliate programs* which pay you a *recurring income*.

This is one way for you to earn money on autopilot. You will keep making money as long as your referred users stay with the company. Of course, quality of the product (**again**) plays a significant role, as nobody will stick to a shoddy product or brand. This is why companies offer recurring commissions; they have a lot of trust in their own product.

Now, I'm *not saying that recurring income is better* than a single affiliate payout because both have their pros and cons.

Let me straightforwardly explain recurring affiliate commissions.

WHAT IS A RECURRING AFFILIATE COMMISSION?

When you recommend a user to buy a product (usually a membership program or multiple-time product) which requires a recurring monthly payment, you will earn **another commission** when the user **makes the next payment**.

Some companies offer recurring commissions for a *fixed time* (e.g., one year) while some offer the same commissions for a *lifetime*. It all depends upon the company's marketing policies.

In this chapter, I will share some of the *best available affiliate programs which offer recurring commissions* and could potentially **be a goldmine** for you and your affiliate marketer friends.

BEST AFFILIATE PROGRAMS WITH RECURRING COMMISSIONS:

I will start the list based on products which **I use**. Also, I have researched about a few products that could also be beneficial for you.

LeadPages

LeadPages is the **topmost tool for internet marketers**. The service lets anyone create a landing page within minutes and add it to their preferred platform (including WordPress, Drupal and all the other popular platforms you can think of).

I have been using them for over a year, and it's a great investment for an end user. At the same time, **they offer an affiliate program which lets you earn a lifetime commission of 30%.**

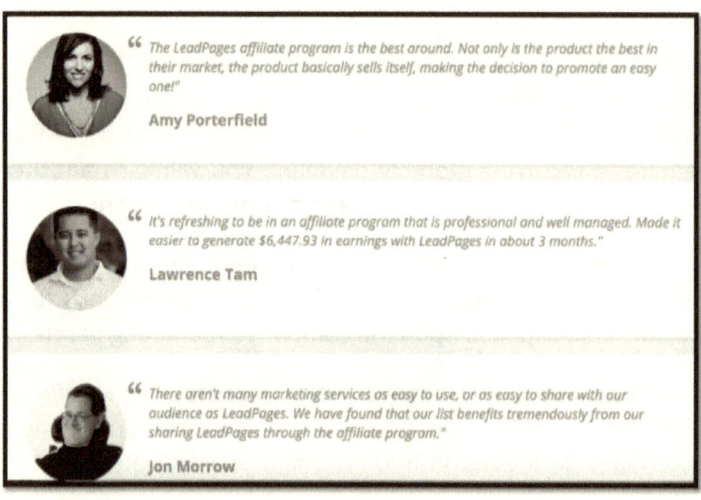

This works out really well for a marketer when referred users sign up for their monthly billing cycle.

Their affiliate team is also **very responsive** and will offer you all the marketing materials (such as *swipe copies* and *social media updates)* for you to drive sales traffic.

Their affiliate program is only available for **current LeadPages customers**. This actually makes sense because you can't really write genuine reviews for a product which you haven't used.

> Join LeadPages Affiliate Program: http://www.shoutmeloud.com/recommended/leadpages

AWEBER

> **Recurring Income**
>
> When someone you refer to us orders an account, you'll earn 30% not only on the initial sale, but also on any recurring payments they make.
>
> Example:
>
> You refer Joe to us, and he signs up at $19.00 per month. Each month Joe uses AWeber, you'll earn $5.70.
>
> After a year, you've made $68.40. After 2 years, $136.80. 3 years? $205.20. And so on as long as Joe continues to use his account.
>
> And that's just one account!

Aweber is one of the oldest and most popular email marketing tools for bloggers and affiliate marketers. They recently integrated the **segmentation feature** which is one of **the top things to do** for *high conversions*.

Aweber also offers a lucrative *30% lifetime commission* to their affiliates.

Getting users onboard is easy as they offer a free 30-day trial, which is usually compelling enough for users to give it a shot.

And let me tell you, **you won't be disappointed** with their email marketing solution. They have everything you need in a *modern* email marketing service for your business to function properly.

To me, an affiliate lifetime commission of 30% *sounds like a win-win*.

The only **downside is their payment method.** They still offer the old-school paper check and have yet to integrate any new payment methods.

Join Aweber Affiliate Program: http://www.shoutmeloud.com/recommended/Aweber/

GetResponse

GetResponse is one of the top alternatives to Aweber.

They too, have a great product and might even have a *slight* edge over Aweber when it comes to commission amount.

They offer **33% lifetime commission** which is *awesome* as it is better than the industry standard. They also offer a 30-day free trial.

It's a good email marketing tool which you can feel comfortable promoting.

- Minimum Payout: $50
- Payout method: Check & PayPal

Join GetResponse Affiliate Program: http://www.shoutmeloud.com/recommended/Getresponse/

ElegantThemes Affiliate Program (WordPress Themes & Plugins):

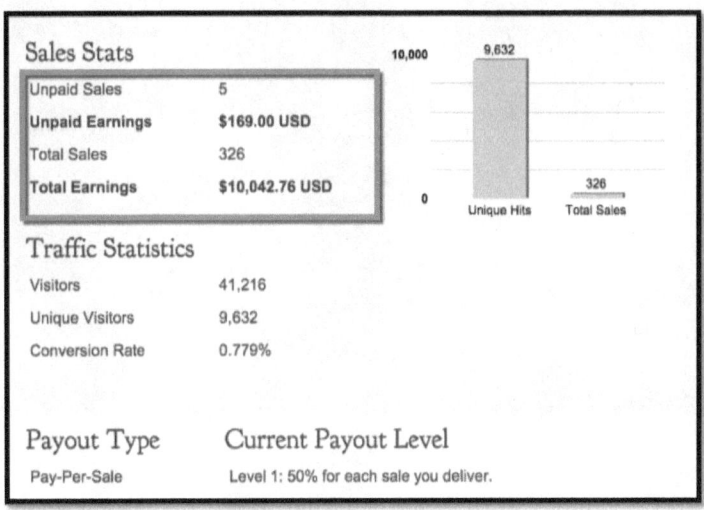

This is not a *typical* **residual income affiliate program.**

ElegantThemes offers premium WordPress themes and plugins. They pay a **50% commission to their affiliates**, and you will also get paid when your referred users *renew their license*.

I really like their affiliate program because of the high commission rate.

- Payment method: Paypal

Join Elegant Themes Affiliate Program: http://www.shoutmeloud.com/recommended/Elegent/

ThriveThemes

ThriveThemes offers an amazing suite of products for WordPress bloggers and internet marketers. Their themes and plugins are **built for conversion optimization**, and they are one of the hottest selling products on the market.

They offer **50% commission/sale & 25% recurring lifetime commission**. And they have a great reputation, so promoting them is easy.

- Payment mode: Paypal

Join Thrive Themes Affiliate Program: http://www.shoutmeloud.com/recommended/Thrivethemes/

SocialPilot

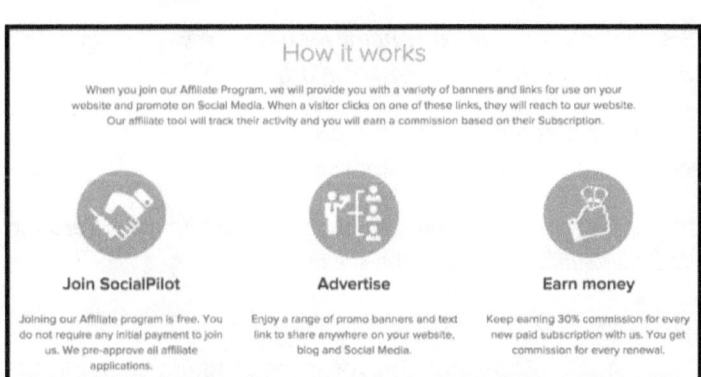

SocialPilot is a social media automation tool which is **widely popular** among bloggers and entrepreneurs.

It helps you in **scheduling updates** on *multiple social media accounts* and also allows you to automate by **auto-publishing using RSS**. I have been using them for a while, and it is safe to say that this is one of the *best social media affiliate programs* available, now that the Bufferapp affiliate program has retired.

They offer a *30% recurring lifetime commission* which is pretty great as they have a "free to pro" plan which is easy to get converters. You will get paid when users **upgrade from a free to a paid account**.

- Payout method: PayPal
- Minimum Payout: $25

Join SocialPilot Affiliate Program: http://www.shoutmeloud.com/recommended/SocialPilot/

(Get $10 as free signup bonus)

More residual income programs:

*("Residual income" is another name for **recurring income** where you earn passive income with no more effort)*

Here are some more affiliate programs which offer residual income that you can sign up for right away.

(Since you are smart, you should always read about the product and affiliate information on the site itself)

- Snip.ly: **20% recurring commission**
- LiquidWeb: **5% monthly recurring commission on dedicated hosting**
- RoseHosting: **50% first month sale + 20% monthly commission on VPS hosting.**
- Shopify Affiliate Program: **20% recurring income**

(I will keep updating the list as I discover more such profitable programs in various niches)

FAQs About Affiliate Marketing

So there it is. Now you have a basic understanding of what affiliate marketing is all about, how it works, and how you can make money from it.

Now, let me answer some of the most commonly asked questions from webmasters and marketers related to affiliate marketing.

Is affiliate marketing harmful or illegal?

No, it's not. You are merely providing a link to another site. Nothing illegal there.

Affiliate marketing and AdSense: Can we use both?

Yes, you can. Affiliate marketing alone doesn't violate the AdSense TOS.

How do you find affiliate links for a specific product?

Not all companies offer affiliate programs, but for companies that do so, you can always check their website or the FAQ page. Another way is to conduct a simple Google search. For example, search the following on Google:

- "**Product name + Affiliate program**" – Replace "product

name" with the product you are promoting, and you will hit an affiliate landing page.

Many companies use affiliate marketplaces like *ShareASale, CJ, and ClickBank.* They are free to use, and you can go ahead and create a free account.

Is it essential to have a blog for affiliate promotion?

Not necessarily. Though having a blog, in my opinion, is the best way to promote your affiliate links. But you can always use things like paid traffic (PPC) or advertisements to promote an affiliate product. However, this is more like a "hit and run" approach to affiliate marketing. The best way to *make the most* out of being an affiliate marketer is to have a blog that is used for hard and soft promotion.

How much does it cost to join an affiliate program?

There is no charge for joining an affiliate program. However, costs can occur depending on what promotion technique you are using. For example, a blog post doesn't cost a dime, whereas PPC marketing, email marketing, or other advertising methods come for a price.

What are the qualifications to become an affiliate marketer?

There are no qualifications required to become an affiliate marketer. However, good *copywriting* and *marketing skills* can be an *added advantage*.

Are there any programs which automatically convert links into affiliate links?

There are a few networks (like Viglink and Skimlinks) which automatically convert regular links into affiliate links. Since they use Javascript, it's SEO friendly. With these links, you do not need to sign up for an individual affiliate program.

How much money can one make from affiliate marketing?

There is *no limit* to the amount you can earn from affiliate programs. It all depends on which program(s) you are promoting and how many conversions you are making. I started with **$47** as my first affiliate income. Today, I make almost **$4k-$5K/month** by merely promoting products that I use every day.

Alright, I understand what affiliate marketing is all about, but how do I get started?

In this book, I have presented you with valuable information on what you need to do to get started. The only way to *actually* get started is to **start**.

Lucky for you, this book is finished, so you can start right about now!

Disclamer: This book contains affiliate links to products. We may receive a commission for purchases made through these links.

www.ingramcontent.com/pod-product-compliance
Lightning Source LLC
Chambersburg PA
CBHW020924180526
45163CB00007B/2870